Treasures of My Heart

Treasures of My Heart

By

Victoria S. Blake

*For Carson,
May the cherished family memories become the Treasures of your Heart!
Gratefully,
Vicki S. Blake
2019*

A Note to the Reader

Great care has been taken to present the voices of the characters in this story as authentic for the late 1800's. I was raised in the Pleasant Gardens community. I have the utmost respect for my ancestors and friends who called this area home. They lived here, worked here, laughed here, loved here and died here. I am proud of my heritage. I am proud of our dialect, our "country" ways and most of all to call this place "where I come from."

Treasures of My Heart

© 2015, Victoria S. Blake

www.victoriasblake.blogspot.com

Illustrated by Carly Kauffman

9 8 7 6 5 4 3 2 1

ALL RIGHTS RESERVED. This book contains material protected under International and Federal Copyright Laws and Treaties. Any unauthorized reprint or use of this material is prohibited. No part of this book may be reproduced or transmitted in any form or by any means, electronic or mechanical, including photocopying, recording, or by any information storage and retrieval system without express written permission from the author.

ISBN 978-1507733967

For Brady, Drew and Lukas

Chapter One
The Dining Room

I stood on the front porch as I had done most mornings of my adult life, looking at the beauty surrounding me. The view was striking. Oh, the color of autumn... leaves of orange, red, and yellow against a brilliant blue cloudless sky. It was as if I was trying to imprint the image in my mind of the mountains in their colorful splendor, although I knew I would not forget this moment for the rest of my days. I closed my eyes and stood there; I wanted to be sure I experienced everything. The early morning rain had stopped. I took a deep breath; *I love the smell after a rain.* The air was cool and crisp. The sound of the rushing creek captured my attention as it flowed by my cherished home. The robins chirped in the oak trees. I felt the breeze gently flow against my face. My mind was flooded with memories of my life here: my family, my husband, and my children. What a life I've had and what a wondrous place to live . . . I love these mountains . . . they are sacred to me.

Our home had served in many capacities since my father-in-law, Colonel John Carson, ceremonially felled the first tree that would be used to build the foundation of this plantation home. I thought of him and of my husband, Logan Carson, as I stood there. I thought of all they had built and accomplished in their lives. I have always been proud of my family . . . now I pray; somehow, they would understand what I feel I must do. The wooden planks creaked as I shuffled across the front porch. It was a familiar sound. As I went through the front entrance, my daughter, Margaret, son-in-law, Colonel Peter Sinclair, and granddaughter, Moffitt were waiting to greet me.

"Mother Carson, are you ready?" My handsome son-in-law was so kind and patient with me.

"Yes, Peter, almost. I just want to take one last look around before we go."

He put his arm around my shoulder and smiled. "Of course, I'll start loading some of the boxes . . . you take your time; we're in no hurry, we'll go whenever you're ready. Margaret, you and Moffitt stay with Big Mother. I'll continue packing things up."

"Moffitt, will you hold my hand? You'll steady me as we walk."

Her hands were soft and tender, the hands of innocence. We walked slowly, my gait unsteady and unsure. I'm afraid my age warrants a slower pace these days.

"Big Mother, are you sad to leave your home?"

I stopped and gently cupped her face in my hand, "Few places touch the heart of a person like home. For me, it was a refuge, a shelter away from the world. Nestled here in these mountains, I found peace and sanctuary. You see child, this place is my life. Who I am . . . what I am . . . is because of this home, and the people who lived here before me and with me. It's where my memories were made."

Moffitt's forehead furrowed and her little mouth cocked to one side. I knew my comment was more for me than for a six year old, and I knew I had failed to answer her question.

"Come, child, I will try to explain." We all walked down the breezeway or dogtrot* as it is called, and turned left into one of the largest rooms of this old house, the dining hall. This room had always been a gathering place for the home's inhabitants. Steadying myself with my wooden cane, I slowly shuffled around the room. The smell of old fires and ashes in the fireplace filled the room. I ran my hand across the wall near the door. The walls were painted pale blue with streaks of dark grey, the artwork of a former boarder, an itinerant preacher, who felt the faux graining effect might give the room character. I guess there's truth in the old saying, 'beauty is in the eye of the beholder.' Single hung windows flanked the fireplace and framed the view that overlooked the creek and distant farmland. I stood silently and stared out the window . . . remembering.

"Are there memories in here, Big Mother?" Moffitt asked. She looked up at me with her blue eyes sparkling while her small fingers twirled her long hair, a characteristic she inherited from her mother.

My mind was turning over and over. Where do I begin? I thought. "Yes, many memories," I answered. "This dining room may just look like a place to eat, Moffitt, but it was an extraordinary room. Many years ago, around 1793, your great-grandfather, Colonel John Carson, chose this very place to settle his family. He built this house and brought his family to live here."

I walked to the center of the room carefully dodging the numerous boxes of packed linens and dishes. "As the story goes, in the middle of this room was a long walnut dining table which held a blue and white platter as its centerpiece.

This platter was very precious to your great-grandmother, Mary. She was the second wife of your great-grandfather, John, and the mother of your grandpa, Logan. When she married Great-Grandpa John, she moved to this house. Logan told me she wrapped the platter very carefully in a soft quilt and carried it on her lap while she rode in a horse-drawn wagon. Her first act as the new mistress of the house was to place that platter on the center of the dining table. She loved this community. Until her arrival, this area was called Garden Hill. But once she placed her platter on the table, she announced it would now be called, Pleasant Gardens. To this day, it is still the name of our community. So you see, Moffitt, this is no ordinary room... the story of our family began here."

I studied every inch of this room. I was flooded with memories. I could almost smell fresh bread baking and taste the sorghum molasses and fresh churned butter of our morning ritual. Oh, how I loved our family celebrations there... especially Christmas, and the birthdays of my children. This room was where we discussed our troubles and celebrated the milestones of our life. But... no more. I took a deep breath and bit my trembling lip. I closed my eyes, afraid the tears would never stop should I give them freedom.

"Now help me, Moffitt," I whispered. "It's time to go."

"No, Big Mother," Moffitt pleaded. "Please tell me more of your memories. I love to hear your stories."

"All homes have stories, child. As you grow older and live your life, you will make some of your own."

Chapter Two
The Parlor

We walked hand in hand across the dogtrot, and I could almost feel the breeze of history hit me in the face. I beamed as I remembered the faces of my daughters sitting by a blazing fire on a cold winter's night, drinking warm cocoa and sharing the day's events. Not all memories in that room were joyful, but most of them had happy endings.

I walked toward the front of the room and gently stroked the wavy beveled glass of the window panes. "Little one, this room was the parlor, by far the most grand and beautiful room in this house."

You would never know it now. The room was empty. No longer did it hold the beautifully upholstered sofas and chairs in colors of burgundy, creamy white and sage green. The beaded fire screen*, the wool rugs, the hand woven tapestry curtains . . . all gone. As little ones often do, Moffitt ran around and began dancing in the vacant room.

"What stories happened in here, Big Mother?"

"Well, let's see in this room . . ." I stopped for a moment as the thoughts in my mind fought to be the most remembered. "Oh child, there are just too many to count, and we don't have time to tell them all."

"Please, Big Mother. I'm begging to hear one."

"All right then, let me think, it's hard to know where to begin; there are so many." I paused momentarily and then asked, "Would you like to hear about weddings, duels or the raiders of the civil war?"

Margaret smiled as we watched Moffitt. Her impish eyes darted back and forth and then she said, "Why don't you tell me a little about each one. At the end, I'll tell you which story I want to hear more about." I grinned and shook my head at her; she was a smart little thing. I then began the account of my life as best as I could remember it.

"One of my favorite memories of this room was when your Grandpa Logan and I were married. I was much younger and less wrinkled then," I said coyly. "After a few months of courtship, he asked my father for my hand in marriage. Of course, my family was delighted for me to marry into the Carson family; everybody around here knew of the Carsons. Great-Grandpa John had been to Charleston and had purchased yards and yards of ivory satin for me and some pale yellow linen cloth for the dress of my bridesmaid. He gave me the fabric as an act of love and approval of our marriage. I was so grateful for his

generosity and kindness. I worked day and night sewing by hand for my wedding; it took weeks to complete the dresses. Kadella helped with the intricate and tedious embroidery. She was a wonderful seamstress and a beloved servant of the Carson family. Finally, my wedding gown was complete with delicate lace details and it fit me like a glove. Our spring wedding was beautiful... the weather perfect. We were married right here in this parlor. Grandpa Logan's sister, Matilda, was my attendant. She carried a bouquet of freshly picked yellow daisies that perfectly matched the color of her floor-length linen dress. And me, I carried my favorite flowers, white magnolia blossoms. If I close my eyes, I can still smell them. I paused momentarily and breathed a sigh and smiled. Your Grandpa Logan said I was his princess. And he... well, he was my prince." I walked toward the window and peering out, I added, "We held a grand party right here on the front lawn. I am proud to say that people traveled from miles around to witness and celebrate the wedding ceremony of Logan and Mary Carson. It was one of the happiest days of my life."

Moffitt jumped up and pretended to fix her veil and carry an imaginary bouquet. "Did you walk like this, Big Mother?" she asked as she demonstrated the one step promenade down the make-believe wedding aisle.

I winked at her and replied, "Something like that."

"One of my favorite women and servants of the house, Aunt Lucindy was there. She graciously blessed us with an old African marital blessing, a libation. It was a special event in African culture, the ritual of pouring libation is an important and essential ceremonial tradition and a way of giving honor to the ancestors. In Africa, ancestors are highly respected; they are invited to participate in all public or family functions. She offered a prayer calling them to attend by sprinkling special oil and asking God to bless our marriage.

It's important to respect your elders, child. Remember that. It was a special time on the plantation; our life was good."

As I stood there lost in my memories, Moffitt quickly reminded me of our agreement. "Tell the next one Big Mother, I am waiting to see which story I want to know more about."

"Moffitt," Margaret scolded, "You're wearing Mother out."

"I'm fine right now, Margaret. You're sweet to be concerned."

I hesitated for a moment . . . my mind searching for the proper way to share this next story.

"Let's see now, in this parlor the Carson family waited to hear the fate of their beloved Samuel Carson, Grandpa Logan's older brother. He died a few years before Grandpa Logan and I were married, so I did not have the privilege of knowing him personally. I do know he was intelligent, 'sharp as a tack' your Grandpa Logan would say, and like your great-grandpa, John, he was involved in politics. Your Grandpa Logan loved him so much. He told me he was a handsome man; I've seen pictures, he did have beautiful brown curls and a big toothy smile that Logan said just made you want to trust him before you ever knew him. Samuel also had a beautiful voice I was told; you know a voice that roused the spirit in your soul? Great-Grandpa John would say he got the 'glory bumps' when Samuel would sing.

"I believe Samuel to be a gentleman who followed something called the "code of chivalry," which was a very strict way things were to be done properly. Some men observed chivalry occasionally, as it suited them, but for Samuel, it was a way of life. The story goes that during a bitter political campaign, Dr. Robert Vance, insulted Great-Grandpa John by calling him a "Tory," a British sympathizer. Seeing that Great-Grandpa John was too old and feeble to fight for himself, Samuel knew he must defend his honor and the Carson name, so he challenged Mr. Vance to a duel. Now dueling was illegal in North Carolina, but not in South Carolina. So right across the border on Saluda Mountain, Samuel and Dr. Vance fought their fight. There was a man, Davy Crockett was his name, and he traveled with Samuel to the duel. Have you ever heard of him?"

Jumping up and down, she squealed, "Yes, Big Mother, I have; we studied about him in school. He was at the Alamo, right?"

"Yes, he was. Very good. I'm glad you're listening to your teachers. He was an avid and keen frontiersman, very active politically and also a dear friend of Samuel's. Your great-grandparents were so distraught and worried about Samuel. One can only imagine how difficult that must have been for them ... wondering if Samuel would live or die. Grandpa Logan said the suspense was horrible. However, late in the day Davy Crockett rode hard and long to deliver the good news, 'The victory is ours!', which meant Samuel had survived. Although he had won the duel, his victory was not jubilant. Being such a compassionate person, the killing of another man haunted him the rest of his life. He and his family eventually left Pleasant Gardens with Davy Crockett by his side. I understand they moved out west where Samuel continued his political ventures and became the First Secretary of State for the Republic of Texas. And his friend, Mr. Crockett, well ... sadly, he died at the legendary battle at the Alamo."

"Was the Alamo during the Civil War?" Moffitt asked.

"No, no darlin'," I responded, "The Civil War came in the 1860's; the Alamo was in 1836."

Moffitt was a good listener, paying close attention to both stories I had shared about the parlor. The sadness of the last story had left everyone rather quiet. Of course, Moffitt quickly fixed that.

"Big Mother, the civil war was a long time ago. Do you still remember much about it?" she asked.

"Yes, Moffitt, I'm afraid I do; I remember it like it was yesterday as a matter of fact. Which brings me to the last story from which you may choose? It's the story of General Stoneman's Raiders." I hesitated. I knew if I shared this memory, I must choose my words most carefully.

Margaret had been quiet during all of my stories . . . until now. "You see, Moffitt, Your Aunt Mary and I were very young when the Raiders came through Pleasant Gardens. Your Grandpa Logan and Big Mother were living here along with our school teacher, Miss Emma Rankin. It was in this parlor that we watched Union soldiers crawl in and out of our windows ransacking our beloved home."

Moffitt watched as Margaret walked over to the dog trot area. "It was here that those callous blue coats rode horses with their ironclad hoofs across our hand-hewn pine floors." She pointed to a deep mark in the floor. "See right here, this scratch is from that frightful day," as she gingerly rubbed her fingers over the mark as I too had done many times in my life when I remembered that day."

"What do you mean, Mother?" Moffitt rushed over to see the marred floor and with a look of genuine bewilderment asked, "But, why? Why would someone damage our floors?"

"It was a long time ago, child, but those memories are etched in my mind," Margaret added. "Perhaps it's best not to share these memories. Hearing them might cause you to have a resentful spirit toward others. We must dwell on the good in our lives, not the bad. Don't you agree, Big Mother?"

"Margaret is right. Perhaps it best to not share this story."

"Tell me about it Big Mother . . . or you tell it, Mother!" she pleaded, "I've made up my mind, this is the story I want to hear," Moffitt said emphatically. "Please tell me. I want to hear why those men came here and ruined our floors."

Margaret raised her eyebrows and pointed to a short tower of stacked chairs in the corner of the parlor. "Well, run get a chair; there are two or three stacked up ready for your father to load. This one is a long one; we will need to sit down for this story."

Moffitt hurriedly skipped over and grabbed a ladder-back woven chair and carried it back for her mother. Being such a caring and thoughtful child, she ran back and retrieved another one for me. She helped guide me to sit down and then curled up at our feet. Her big blue eyes stared up at us with such anticipation. How could one possibly say no to that face?

"Big Mother, perhaps you would like for me to share this one?" Margaret asked.

"Of course . . . that might be best," I replied.

* * * * * *

"Well child . . . I was about your age; my sister, you're aunt Mary and I started our day as usual."

"'Hurry Margaret,' Mary urged, 'breakfast is almost ready.' Mary always got up before me.

"'Go ahead, sis, I'll be right there!' I answered rubbing the sleep from my eyes. I loved my quiet alone time in my bedroom in the morning. I would lazily lie there planning my day.

"Spring in Western North Carolina was as close to paradise as one could get. The smell of honeysuckle and lilac filled the air. The glorious azaleas were in full bloom . . . colors of pink, deep orchid and white surrounded our home and made a nice complement to the magnolia trees on our plantation. The forsythias were bright yellow and the grass, tender and lime green. The English boxwoods were putting out their spring shoots . . . they would need trimming soon. As I lay there, I heard the rushing waters of Buck Creek outside my bedroom window. It was too early for an open window at night, but I knew it would not be long until the muggy, humid, thick air of summer would fill our home. However, on that particular morning the temperature was perfect. In the distance, I heard the slave help singing as they were heading out to the fields.

I slid out of bed when Aunt Lucindy came by our room.

'Can I he'p ya get ready for breakfas'?' she asked.

"I loved Aunt Lucindy; she was very old. She had been in the Carson family for many, many years."

"'No, thank you, Aunt Lucindy... I'll get up- I promise.'

'Ok child. Now you herry up though! You got to eat breakfas' and school starts shotly,' she said as she quietly hobbled back down the stairs.

"There was fresh water in my pitcher on the washstand. It was cold but pure and crystal clear... straight from the creek. After I had washed my face, I dressed myself –all except my shoes. I just couldn't get that buttonhook* to work that morning! Buttoning my shoes was always a hard task for me.

"All of a sudden I heard a stern determined voice, 'Miss Margaret Carson, are you planning to join us for breakfast?' I looked up and saw a tall, thin lady standing in the doorway. Her gray woolen dress fit her frame neatly, not too snug, but not slouchy. If there was one thing Miss R was not, it was slouchy. Her dark hair was rolled in a tight bun and her wire rimmed glasses were small for her face. Her arms were akimbo, and her feet planted firmly at my doorway.

" 'Yes ma'am, Miss R, I'm a coming, I promise, I'm coming right now,' I answered without delay.

"Miss R was Miss Emma Rankin, our schoolteacher. Most days, the only folks in our home were Big Mother, Grandpa Logan, Miss R, Mary, and me. Sometimes other children in the community attended school with us in our home. It was dependent on the farming chores and harvest time. We had occasional boarders, but not at this time. Although once there had been over 65 servants or slaves that helped with the chores on the plantation, now only around 20 remained: Among them were Nance and her children, Aunt Hannah and Jeff and their children, and Aunt Lucindy and Paddy.

" 'Miss Margaret Carson . . . it is most ill-mannered to keep others waiting. Hurry child!' instructed Miss R. Her lips were pursed, and her brown eyes were squinting as she turned and quickly walked toward the stairs.

" 'What a problem I have!' I said aloud, although no one was there to hear my comment. 'I can go down to breakfast without my boots on or I can be late . . . oh well, no boots it is!' I didn't want to be late for biscuits and molasses, side meat and fresh eggs. Who would?

"I headed downstairs boots in one hand and buttonhook in the other. Big Mother was always a proper Southern lady. She came to breakfast dressed beautifully in a dark green cotton dress with big puffy sleeves with hand-stitched white Battenberg lace trim . . . on time, I might add. When she saw my dilemma, her face fell; she seemed most disappointed at my appearance.

" 'I'm sorry, mother,' I said while entering the dining room. 'I've tried but I just can't get this buttonhook to workin' this morning.'

" 'Here, here child, let Lucindy he'p.' Aunt Lucindy knelt down and in a matter of seconds, my boots were properly buttoned, and I took my seat at the breakfast table. Aunt Lucindy could do anything.

"Just as we finished saying grace, there was a loud rapping at the front door of the dining room. Miss R excused herself from the table and quickly jumped up to answer the visitor's persistent knocking. I heard the deep voice of a man say, 'Morning ma'am, sorry to come by so early but, is Mr. Carson home?'

"Big Mother rose to join Miss R. She cordially and calmly addressed the man, 'No sir; I am afraid he's already out and about this morning. I'm his wife; my name is Mary Carson, and this is Miss Emma Rankin, our school teacher. How may we be of help to you, sir?'

" 'Well, ma'am,' The officer respectfully removed his hat and placed it in front of his chest. 'You see, ladies, I'm Lieutenant Samuel Neal. My men and I are tired, ma'am, and we haven't eaten a full meal in days. If you could offer some food for some hungry soldiers this morning, we'd be ever indebted to you for your kind hospitality.'

" 'Of course, Lieutenant, please do come in.' Big Mother motioned for me. I came to her at once.

" 'Run tell Hannah we have a few extra mouths to feed this morning. Hurry now, these fine men are starving! We must see to them right away.'

"Big Mother welcomed the strangers into our home like they were long lost family. 'Now don't you worry,' she said, 'I'll have Hannah fix you good men something to eat. We have plenty.' About five or six confederate soldiers entered the house and took their places around our dining room table. They looked weary; their wretched gray uniforms were dusty, tattered and worn. Nevertheless, we loved to see them coming; I felt safer when those soldiers were nearby. The Lieutenant bowed his head and prayed the most humble prayer, thanking God for our home and generosity . . . and several times for the food.

"Aunt Hannah served them a delicious hot breakfast of sawmill gravy and home-canned sausage, cathead biscuits and freshly gathered farm eggs. How Aunt Hannah made enough food for unexpected company on the spur of the moment always amazed me. The men complimented her cooking the whole time they were eating, although I'm not sure they even tasted the food. They gulped it down so quickly.

"Miss R sat ever so straight in her chair, her posture perfect. Looking out over the top rim of her glasses, she questioned the lieutenant, 'Sir, please tell us any news. We hear...uh, stories...rumors really, that there may be Union soldiers coming closer. Is there any truth to that?'

" 'Yes Ma'am, I'm afraid it is. Even though I feel the end of the war is at hand, there are still offshoots of the Union army that are ravaging homesteads in surrounding counties. Their stealing livestock and doing great damage. I'm afraid it's only a matter of time 'til they come through here.'

"Big Mother's face was easy to read. She put her hand over her mouth and hung on his every word.

"Miss R continued her inquisition, 'We've been lucky here; we've had very little direct battles in this area. I hope they change their course. Surely they will. You don't think we are in any real danger, do you, Lieutenant Neal?'

"The Lieutenant looked directly at Big Mother, 'I trust you folks will make necessary and appropriate plans. You know what to do, I'm sure. Protect what you have, Mrs. Carson, the Union is comin'. Tell your husband and anybody else that has hands and can work to make ready. But, make no mistake...they're comin'.'

"With that comment, the Lieutenant ordered his men to excuse themselves from the table. He stopped long enough to express his appreciation for their breakfast, and they were off. With urgency in their steps, the men mounted their horses. I watched them ride off until I could no longer see them on the horizon.

"Now normally we headed straight upstairs to our classroom after breakfast, 'Education first!' Big Mother would always say.

"Nothing came before school. However, that was not the case that day. Big Mother, Miss R, Aunt Hannah, Aunt Lucindy, Mary, and I gathered around our dining room table. I remember Big Mother was breathing heavily, excited, but quietly determined in her directions. Her first instructions were clear, 'Mary, darlin', run now, go quickly. Find your father! Tell him to come to the house at once, tell him it is very important. Hurry now child . . . run! And Hannah, you go find Jeff and Paddy. Tell them to gather all the help they can find – tell thim to start digging a big hole out back in the vegetable garden. Please hurry, Aunt Hannah! Miss Rankin, you and Margaret will help me. We will go all through the house – anything of value - bring it here to the dining room table. Hurry now, everyone . . . Hurry!' You could tell Big Mother meant business. Everyone jumped without once questioning her authority.

"In a matter of minutes, the house was filled with people, everyone frantically working to protect our home and its belongings.

" 'Missus Carson, if'n you don't mind,' Paddy said, 'I'll go and try to he'p with dat hole. We got several hams and side meat we ought to try and save.'

" 'Yes, Paddy! Do that. Thank you; that's good thinking!'

" 'I'll help!' Miss Rankin jumped up, rolling up the long sleeves of her dress as she followed after Paddy.

"'No, ma'am, Miss R,' said Paddy, 'Dat's man's work, Miss R, I couldn't let you he'p me with dat t'day.'

" 'Nonsense! There's no time for that kind of talk, Paddy; we all have to help.' Ignoring his pleas, she nearly knocked him down while she pushed by him in the doorway of the dining hall.

"Miss Rankin had a tin box in her hands. I'm not sure what she had in that box, but I would imagine it was money she was burying. Miss R was a strong, healthy lady, but the physical work of digging a 6'x6'x2' hole deep enough for Poppa's confederate money, a few hams, and some treasures from the house, along with her little tin box had left her hands bleeding and blistered, though she

never complained for a minute. That entire day we gathered our things, anything of value we buried, hid, or gave to Hannah or Lucindy to hide in their homes.

"Later that night as Mary and I lay in our beds, I overheard Big Mother and Grandpa Logan 'discussing' our dilemma. I say 'discussing' because Big Mother always said folks that love one another shouldn't argue. And she is right. Our bedroom was right above the dining room, so it wasn't hard to hear their conversation. 'Logan, you must leave,' Big Mother pleaded. 'You must not be here when the Yankees come. They will take you prisoner; I couldn't bear to see that happen. Listen to me, Logan, I'm begging you, you must leave us and hide close by until the danger has passed.'

" 'No, Mary!' Grandpa Logan replied. 'I won't leave you and the girls. I can't leave you alone, and I don't want to leave our home.' I could hear Grandpa Logan pounding his fist on the dining room table. 'My father, a brave and noble man, the Colonel John Carson, loved this house, as do I. I must stay and defend it. I won't run! I can't run off and hide; try to understand!'

"Big Mother's voice suddenly got quieter, but I could still hear her clearly. 'I understand your devotion and loyalty to us, Logan, but it's our only chance of holding onto our home. The Yankees will take you from us if they find you,' Big Mother explained. 'Please, Logan, please leave, I beg you. Just go into the woods with the horses; stay there until the threat is over. If you love us, Logan, you will do as I ask. Please Logan . . . go.'

"Poor Poppa. He felt compelled to stay and protect his home and family. But honestly, he knew he could do more to save and protect us by being absent when the Yankees arrived. *Maybe those Union soldiers would feel sorry for us . . . just women and children in the house . . .* I thought to myself. Finally, after much deliberation, Grandpa Logan conceded; the plan was decided if those Yankees came, he would hide with the horses in the edge of the woods.

"The next morning, I did not need to be coaxed out of bed. Everyone was up at the break of day, waiting, watching, and dreading the thought of what might come our way. Everyone meant Big Mother, Grandpa Logan, Miss R, Mary, and me. Aunt Lucindy was in her cabin, and Aunt Hannah and her children were in their cabin. We had done everything we could think of to protect our home and land. Unfortunately, our wait was short-lived. In the early morning hours, we heard the sound of running feet. It was Aunt Hannah's son.

"'The Yankees are comin'! The Yankees are comin'!' he yelled. We quickly ran up the stairs and out the door onto the outside upper porch, or veranda. From that vantage point, one could see for miles.

"As the regiment came closer, Miss R said, 'Come on Margaret, we shall go meet them. Shall we let these men pass without finding out who they are? I think not!' She grabbed my hand and down the stairs we went. With a resolute look on her face and an unyielding gait to her walk, we headed straight toward those soldiers. As we approached them, she continued talking with fervor, 'We will tell them we are alone and have nothing to give. Surely, they will not hurt two innocent ladies with small children, little girls at that!' she continued, trying to convince herself and anyone else that was within earshot. As we grew closer, we could see the men were wearing the gray uniforms of the honorable confederate army.

"Miss R sighed in relief, 'Oh Captain, sir, I'm glad it's you!' Miss R held onto me tightly. 'We thought you were the Yankees!'

"'No, ma'am, but be aware, they are close behind us, please, ma'am, you all are in danger,' he pled with us, 'You must leave this plantation. You and your family cannot stay here.'

"Biting her lip she listened intently and then answered him, 'We have nowhere to go, sir.' Miss R stared down the road as though she could see right through them. 'Please sir, I wonder, could you . . . would you stay and give us some protection?'

"'But ma'am, these are not ordinary Union soldiers,' he added, 'they're renegade riders whose sole intent is to demoralize the Southern way of life and destroy property, steal livestock and take prisoners. Don't you understand?'

"'Yes sir, I understand,' Miss R looked down at the ground answering him in a softer and more polite voice, 'We have been fortunate to have been spared the brunt of the war. We have done all we know to do to protect this home and our meager belongings.' Looking up at the Captain, her voice suddenly became more confident and assured, 'Sir, God is no respecter of persons . . . if it is His will and the Yankees come here . . . Our Lord will protect us.'

"Looking down from atop his black horse, his expression crestfallen, the tired Captain responded, 'I'm sorry we are unable to stay and help protect you and this lovely home,' he continued, 'but we have our orders, and we must travel on to our destination. We will pray for your safety, ma'am.' He tipped his hat as he and the other soldiers rode off heading westward. We stood there and watched our would-be protectors ride away until the dust settled on that old dirt road. I was scared. I knew Miss R was too.

"The next couple of days were filled with anxiety. The rumors continued to pour in, each one supporting the fact that the dreaded Yankees were indeed coming and unless the Lord intervened, they would come right through the Carson plantation.

"One Sunday morning in April, a beautiful spring day, right before daylight our fears came to fruition. Miss R came rushing into our bedroom, 'Hurry girls, get your clothes on. The Yankees are getting closer!' Big Mother and Grandpa Logan were already up. While we were putting on our clothes, we overheard them talking about a letter Miss R had received in the wee hours of the morning. A family member from Salisbury had sent the letter by horseman to warn her of the Raiders and what they might do should they come through our area. It seemed sure; the Union renegades were coming our way. Last minute items were taken to the freshly dug hole in the vegetable garden. Paddy and Jeff placed vegetables and sod back over it, so as to try and disguise its location. Aunt Hannah and her children hurriedly carried the rest of our clothes and left them in an abandoned cabin on the outskirts of our property in an attempt to salvage some of them.

"It was the Lord's Day, and as was every Sunday morning, we headed to church. As I sat reverently in that wooden structure, I kept thinking about our home, wondering if the Yankees had arrived. *Would they destroy our home? Would they hurt us?* It was hard to pay attention that morning, but I listened as our blessed pastor tried to give us hope and strength with his sermon.

He told us of the mighty power of God, reminding us that there were lions in the way, but God could shut the lion's mouths as he had done in Daniel's time. His words were spiritual food for our hungry souls. And as always, we found peace and solace in God's Word.

"Monday passed without incident. The waiting was intense and exhausting. Every outside sound would bring one of us to a window, peering out to see who was approaching. About noon on Tuesday, our long wait was over. As the clock struck noon, the sound of a retreating horseman could be heard screaming at the top of his lungs, 'The Yankees are just across the river!'

"Big Mother urged Grandpa Logan to leave, 'Please Logan, Please go now. You've done all you can to help us. Please, Logan, take the horses and go!'

"Grandpa Logan reached for Big Mother, then Mary and lastly me. I had never been hugged so tightly. 'You girls, be strong and brave. Help your mother. Do everything she says. You hear? I love you . . . I love you all,' he said. I will never forget his pitiful expression . . . I knew his heart was breaking.

" 'I love you, Poppa,' I said, 'Don't worry. We are brave.'

"Grandpa Logan smiled ever so slightly, then turned and started toward the back door; he stopped for just a second, tears flowing from his eyes. 'I'm praying, Mary, you pray too!'

" 'Always,' Big Mother replied.

"Our friends of the Confederacy had not stayed to protect us, and Poppa had left us, as did most of all the servants of the plantation. Big Mother picked me up holding me as close as she could to her chest. I could feel her heart beating through her dress. Miss R grabbed my sister's hand, 'Not so tight Miss R; my fingers are turning white,' Mary said, as she tried to loosen Miss R's grip.

"We stood courageously on the front porch hoping they would see we were no threat to them. I guess we thought our mere presence would keep them out, but as I looked behind me . . . men were coming in the back door, crawling in these parlor windows, going upstairs and rudely pushing right by us in the doorway. It was during that initial entry that the blue intruder and his mangy old horse scratched these floors. He grinned at the mark it left in the dogtrot, he almost seemed proud of it. Such reckless abandon. Such disregard for our home. It was sad.

"Their attacks came in droves. When one would end we would have peace for a few short hours, and then another band of those heartless marauders would come through. They were ruthless. I heard them curse and question Big Mother. I was afraid for her. You see Moffitt, Big Mother was the best mother anyone could ask for. She was usually so tender and compassionate for others. However, I soon learned my mother was audacious as well. She stood her ground and answered those blue intruders with a zeal I had never seen in her before. Those Yankees were competent in their attack, completely ransacking our house. Pulling drawers out from bedroom dressers or breaking down locked doors, anything to bring destruction.

"I remember Mary telling Big Mother she thought she was brave. Big Mother just smiled at Moffitt and said, "Sometimes child, life leaves you no choice. I could be brave because I knew God was with us. And the Good Book says, 'if God is with us, who can be against us?' I had faith that He would protect and deliver us."

Margaret continued. "The day had been long but now the first night of their campaign was upon us. The Yankees made camp outside our house on every side. As if the day's events were not scary enough, a spring thunderstorm was quickly approaching over the mountain. The lightning added to our terror, and the thunder always brought to mind guns firing. We chose to stay in the sanctuary of the downstairs guest bedroom, right off of the parlor over there. Big Mother thought that would be the safest place. At least if they set fire to our home, we had a chance of escaping out the window of the first floor. We had no light. The candles were locked up in the oak candle press, and we had neither the strength nor means to open it. Those blue coats had taken the keys during their first raid on our house.

" 'Girls, try to sleep,' Big Mother prompted, 'Miss R and I will keep watch. God is with us. Remember the scripture your father taught you; you know, the one to give you assurance when you are afraid.'

"Together, Mary and I quoted the words, 'What time I am afraid, I will trust in Thee.' Although I knew rest would not come easy, in fact, it would be nearly impossible to sleep, we didn't argue with Big Mother. We obeyed.

"As the storm subsided, the pouring rain continued. We heard a gentle tapping on the bedroom window. Big Mother quietly eased the window open. His clothes soaked, Paddy whispered, 'Missus Carson, dey found Mr. C and stole de horses. Dey took him, but dey have turned him loose. I ain't sure why, but dey turned him loose. He wants to know if'n he can come home now?'

" 'No!' Big Mother did not even have to think about her answer. 'Paddy, tell him no, not yet. Please . . . you must tell him to stay in hiding; the Yankees may change their minds.'

" 'Yes, ma'am . . . Missus Carson, I'll tell him. Is you folk ok?' Paddy asked. The rain was worsening. There was a steady stream of water falling from his black felt hat.

"'Yes, Paddy, we are physically okay, just mentally exhausted. They have ransacked our home. Those horrid scoundrels even found a jar of molasses and bag of corn meal and poured it out over everything. What a mess! They're callous, but so far, they have not hurt us. Paddy, please tell Logan we're fine and to stay put.'

"'Yes, ma'am,' Paddy answered, 'I will do jus' dat.'

"The darkness of that night seemed to last an eternity. Aunt Hannah came by right before dawn to find us all huddled together in one room in one bed. 'Come now, Missus Carson, ya'll come to our cabin,' she urged. 'Ya'll come have some breakfas'.'

"Big Mother smiled. 'How kind you are Aunt Hannah. I know you only have your allotment. Are you certain there is enough for your family and all of us?'

"'Shore nuf ma'am. You has always provided for me and my family. If'n I got food, you got food.' she added. She scooped Mary up in her arms and took me by my hand. 'Come on now, Miss R, you and Missus Carson, herry up! Dem marauders is a sleepin' . . . we can go now if'n we herry.'

"'Thank you, Hannah, you are kind. We are so weak from hunger,' Big Mother whispered. 'Now girls, listen . . . we must be silent, don't make a sound. Do you understand?' We nodded and very quietly exited the house through the back door.

"Unbeknownst to Aunt Hannah not all the soldiers were sleeping; someone was assigned to watch our every move. They saw us enter into Aunt Hannah's cabin out back of the main house. I'm sure they knew what we were doing. They had covered every inch of our home; they knew we had no food. We managed to eat what we could before the soldiers came bursting through her door. Fortunately, we were able to grab a few bites before those selfish men finished everything off.

"By the afternoon, our ordeal was almost over. They had done their damage. One last injury remained. That bunch of blue coated thieves had decided to leave, but not before parading all of Grandpa Logan's prize horses around in front of the house. We had been as tough and brave as we could, but when your Aunt Mary saw some big, old, fat Union soldier ride off on the back of her favorite pony, the tears began to flow. Unbelievably, that was not the worst of it. Since they could not find a saddle for our pony, they stole Aunt Lucindy's shawl and used it as a horse blanket on which to ride away.

"Everybody knew about Aunt Lucindy's hand-made shawl. It had covered every newborn on our plantation … free or slave. Not only had Aunt Lucindy helped with the delivery of new babies, she would hold a very special service when the baby was one week old. First, she would cover the baby with the soft shawl. Then she would soak a special leaf and rub it on the baby's belly; she believed the leaf cleansed the inner soul of the child. Then she would take this white powder that looked like flour, and as she threw it to the wind, she would face the east and say: 'For our ancestors of de' distant past.' Then she would turn and face west and say, 'For our recent livin' dead.' She would turn to the north and say, 'For de' livin'.' Then lastly, she would face the south and say, 'For de' unborn.' She would end the blessing by kneeling in prayer and saying, 'May the Lord Jesus bless and protect dis' child all yer days and may ye bring glory and honor to Him. Amen.' I loved to watch her do that.

"The shawl was so special to our family, and those hateful men carried it off. In all my life, I never saw Aunt Lucindy cry, until then.

"Well, regrettably, the renegades came back and made several attempts over the next few days to further scare us and break our spirit. Nevertheless, we persevered and survived."

Our little Moffitt sat with her head bowed, silent. I bent down and picked her up, placing her on my lap. Consoling her, I said, "Like I told you child, it's best not to dwell on sad things. They can haunt you and drown the joy in your heart.

Please remember, Moffitt, try to forget the things folks do that hurt you, forget the sorrows of yesterday, and think on things that are pure and honest. The Good Book says to think on those things. That's what I do."

"Wow! Mother, what a story! Big Mother, I will not be sad, 'cause you and my mother are here, and you're all right. I am happy that you all survived and so did this house, even if they did make a bad mark in our floor," Moffitt replied. Then with a renewed optimism in her voice announced, "And I thought parlors were just for gentleman callers!"

Chapter Three
The Bedroom

While we had shared our parlor stories, my son-in-law had continued packing up the house. The day was passing quickly; it was half past four and our time was drawing to a close.

"Now let's go upstairs, child. It's getting late."

I instructed Margaret and Moffitt to put the chairs back and hand in hand, we climbed the steep staircase.

"Watch your head, Moffitt," I cautioned, "You're getting taller and the header of these stairs is low." Although I don't think she was in danger of bumping her head, she ducked just the same.

"Are there memories in here too, Big Mother?" Moffitt asked.

"Well, as a matter of fact, yes. In here, I dreamed the dreams of a young married woman. Your Grandpa Logan and I would lie awake at night staring out the windows watching the stars. When one would shoot across the sky, we would close our eyes and make our wishes."

My little Moffitt grabbed my hand and squeezed it tightly, "What did you wish for, Big Mother?"

"Lots of things really. Mostly, I dreamt of having lots of children and beautiful grandchildren, like you." I patted the top of her head and stroked her straight, waist length hair.

"Did all your dreams come true?" She looked up at me optimistically with that playful grin. "Well, I have you, don't I?" I replied with a proud smile. Looking around the empty room, I added, "Honestly, most of them did, child. God has been good to me. I've had more blessings than trials."

"We didn't always sleep in here you know. On hot, humid summer nights, we would take our blankets and feather pillows and go sleep on the veranda. There was always a cool breeze blowing by the creek. That same cool breeze turned into bitter cold wind though in the winter months. If it hadn't been for the handmade quilts that the servants made, we would probably have frozen to death.

"Most of the slaves learned the art of quilting from their mothers. Aunt Kadella and Fatima were two of the best quilters anywhere around here. They shared their craft and exceptional skills with their friends and passed down the art to their families. I still have two of their quilts; I treasure them. Moffitt, I want you to take extra special care of them after I'm gone to be with Mr. Jesus. They are priceless to me."

"I will, Big Mother, I'll take good care of them," she said crossing her heart, "I promise. What happened to Aunt Kadella and Fatima?"

"Well, Aunt Kadella lived here on the plantation until she passed. According to what your Grandpa Logan told me, she was a beautiful woman. He told me she was of royal lineage, a princess from the British owned island of Barbados. Because of that, she was treated very well by your great-grandpa John. He built her a little cabin out back on the opposite side of the creek, away from all the other servants. From what I know, she was allowed to quilt, weave and sew most of her days. From a bolt of flowered French fabric, Kadella would cut the flowered pattern, rearrange it to suit her taste, and applique it to a white background. She then quilted the whole thing with thousands of minuscule stitches. It was unique and beautiful. Aunt Kadella did not work in the fields; in fact, the other slaves carried her around on a sedan-chair wherever she went. Even they knew she was different.

Now Fatima was a little different story. I was told she too was believed to be from royal lineage. She came to the plantation by way of Charleston, South Carolina, where Great-Grandpa John had visited and purchased her. Fatima did not speak or write the language of any other slaves on the plantation which made her life here even more difficult. One day an African missionary visited our home. He quickly recognized Fatima's dialect as Arabic and told Great-Grandpa John that he believed her to be a Muslim princess. Later on she left the Carson Plantation and resided at the Green River Plantation down near Rutherfordton, North Carolina. We never saw her again.

These fine women were instrumental in the heritage of quilt making here.

Although they had left their native land at an early age, they could still remember how to do the beautiful stitch work of quilting. They influenced the one quilt that I am most proud of, the quilt top made by Hannah Greenlee. I want you to listen very carefully, Moffitt. It is important for you to understand the significance of this quilt." I walked over to the stack of boxes piled up in the corner of the room. Carefully folded and wrapped in the largest box was the quilt top.

"Look here, what do you see?"

Moffitt looked intently at the colorful, but very mismatched pattern of scraps and material sewn together.

"Well... I see a mess... pieces of material, mostly scraps," she answered. "Bless their hearts, I guess they just had to use the leftover pieces of fabric when they made this one, didn't they?"

"Well, they did get the "leftovers" most of the time, I guess," I answered. "But this particular quilt is sometimes called a 'crazy' quilt. It is very special. You see during the civil war, when slavery was at the very heart of the conflict, there were slaves that desperately longed to be free. Some had very hard lives and were not cared for or treated well; they dreamed of escape from their cruel slave masters. They took their lives in their own hands by trying to leave. Their escape was not always planned; it usually happened at an open opportunity, which left little time to prepare how to survive on their own. Some of the slaves had lived their entire lives in captivity and had no idea of what life was like to be free. Having no money would make it nearly impossible to buy supplies, lodging or clothes. They didn't have guns or weapons with which to hunt for food. However, the hunger in their soul to

be free burned so fiercely, so intensely, that the flight was worth the risk. You can understand their desire to be free, can't you?"

Moffitt nodded her head fervently, "Sure I can!"

I continued my story. "So they became dependent on something called 'The Underground Railroad,' a group of people who would secretly help those slaves that had escaped. Which brings me back to this 'crazy' quilt," I carefully took the quilt top in my hands. "Legend tells us that this quilt helped those who were on the run."

"How did a quilt help people who were in hiding?" Moffitt asked. "Did they use it to hide under or as a covering to stay warm?"

I unfolded the quilt and gently placed it in the middle of the floor.

"No darling, although that would have helped them on a cold winter night, I guess," I said with a chuckle. "Each day quilts like these would be hung outside. It would appear to the plantation owner that it was being placed on the clothesline or tree branch to freshen it in the morning sunlight. But if one looked very carefully at the quilt one would see that all the mismatched scraps of fabric are purposefully sewn together to create a map. Look, Moffitt, do you see these crosses?" I asked, pointing to the embroidered work.

She got down closer to the quilt, "Yes, I do!"

"Those stood for churches in the area that could provide refuge or sanctuary." I pointed to other areas on the quilt. "These stitches represented roads, rivers, creeks, forests, and other landmarks that would give a passing escapee plenty of information on where they could find food, shelter, or clothing. Quilts like these became their lifeline to freedom. This particular quilt took years to complete. A talented girl named Hannah started it. It needs to be finished, perhaps one day it will be. Moffitt, I treasure it. Please make sure to keep it safe."

"I will, Big Mother. You can count on me to protect it," and again she crossed her heart and said, "I promise."

A few quiet moments passed. "I don't understand slavery, Big Mother." Moffitt said softly, almost whispering the words.

I picked my sweet grandchild up and held her close. "Well, this is how I see it, and how I am sure your mother sees it as well. I don't believe that anyone should be indentured to another, and I'm happy that slavery was abolished, it was wrong to buy and sell people. I believe everyone deserves freedom to live their life and make their own choices. Now I know some people will not understand what I am going to tell you. And truthfully, I know this was not the situation at all plantation homes in the south. But here at the Carson House, this is the way I felt about the good people that worked here. These people I loved . . . and I loved them deeply. They were so close to me, as close as family. Their devotion to the Carson family was honorable." I stopped momentarily and took a deep breath. "You see Moffitt, I truly believe when I close my eyes in death and open them in heaven, I will see the face of my savior, Jesus, and then I hope to see my family . . . your Grandpa Logan, my mother and father and all the others that have gone on before me. I look forward to seeing them again. But I also believe I will see the loving faces of my slave families there to welcome me into the pearly gates. I cherished those people and appreciated their service to our family. We couldn't have had a successful plantation without them; their tireless devotion to our family was unique and valuable and I am proud to have known them."

We were suddenly interrupted by Peter.

"Mother Carson? Margaret? Moffitt? Where are you?" Peter called from the foot of the stairs.

"Right here, Daddy. We're upstairs!" Moffitt yelled in reply.

"We're coming, Peter," I answered as I gently placed Moffitt back down on the planked pine floor.

"Don't worry, Big Mother, or be sad. You're coming to live with us. We'll make some great new memories," she said smiling that beautiful Carson smile.

"I'm not sad, my darling Moffitt. Today is just a little bittersweet; change usually is."

As Margaret, Moffitt and I walked outside on the second floor veranda, I continued, "Moffitt, one thing is for sure, when you have lived as long as I have you know that life is all about change. The sooner you realize that fact, the easier it will be to accept the inevitable . . . nothing in life stays the same. The good times cannot stay good all the time, and the bad times will usually get better."

I took a deep breath and let it go slowly. I gazed up at those ancient, rounded, rolling mountains. I listened one last time to Buck Creek rushing over its smooth river rocks. My heart was once again overcome with emotion as the tears flowed down my cheeks. I reached in my pocket for my favorite lace handkerchief. As I wiped my face, I turned to Moffitt. "Listen child, during my lifetime I've seen the beauty of God's sunrise that brings hope of a new day, and I've seen the peace of His sunset at day's end. I've felt the touch of a loving husband's hand and the cry of a newborn baby in my arms. I've witnessed the beautiful seasons the Lord has given us . . . each with its own distinctive beauty. Yes, I've had heartache. There was sickness, war, death, and destruction mixed in there too. But it was the depth of the valleys that made me appreciate the height of the mountaintop. I've been blessed with love in my life. The people that lived here in this house loved each other and cared deeply for others through this journey we call life. That's what makes a family - unconditional love.

You may not always understand the actions of others, but try to love them through the pain. We'll only be held accountable for how we behave; we cannot control the actions of others. Life is short. So love those that love you, and love those that don't. 'Cause that's what the Good Book says to do, and it ain't never wrong."

"Beautifully said, Big Mother." Margaret kissed my forehead.

I knew Moffitt not only was listening, but I believe even though she was very young, she understood what I was saying.

I leaned down and placed both of my hands on the cheeks of her innocent face. "You see, Moffitt, a very smart man once told me, 'a house is just a house - it's a family that will make a house a home.' You remember that as you grow older, child. Family means everything."

I looked around to find my handsome son-in-law smiling and patiently waiting to assist me down the stairs.

"Shall we go, Mother Carson?" He quietly asked as he extended his arm for me to steady myself.

"Yes, Peter, I believe it's time." We walked together down the stairs. Margaret and Moffitt followed close behind. At the foot of the stairs, Peter picked up the last lone box by the door; it held our precious 'crazy' quilt. I stood on the front porch watching my loved ones walk away. Peter reached inside the box and handed Moffitt the 'crazy' quilt top. She pressed it to her chest and carried it with care, ever protecting it from dragging the ground. I knew I could trust her with our family heirloom, she had kept her word; I was proud of her.

I pulled the front door closed and turned the key for the final time. I carefully maneuvered the front steps and slowly walked down the surrey path leaving behind the comfort of my past. I thought of Great-Grandpa John and my dear husband, Logan. At the end of the path, I paused and looked toward the heavens and whispered, "I will love you both . . . always. Please forgive me. I hope you understand the decision I had to make in selling our home. I know, Grandpa John, you always said, 'a house is just a house; it's a family that will make a house a home.' You were right. But now it's time. It's time for a new family to make this house their home. May God bless them and those that will live here."

I breathed a sigh of release. As I leave with my daughter's family, I am resolved. I look forward to the future, but I will not forget my past. I will carry with me eternally these precious memories, for it's in those memories I have found the treasures of my heart.

Glossary

Dogtrot - The breezeway through the center of the house is a unique feature in that the rooms of the house led into this open hallway. This provided a cooler covered area for sitting. The combination of the breezeway and open windows in the rooms of the house created air currents that pulled cooler outside air into the living quarters efficiently in the pre-air conditioning era.

Beaded Fire Screen - The screen began to appear in the 18th century. It is a smaller screen placed on a vertical pole which is mounted on a tripod; placed between a lit fire and occupant of the room, the screen can be adjusted up or down to shield a person's face from the heat. Women wore heavy makeup during this time, and the heat of the fireplace would "melt" the makeup from their faces. The screen helped protect their faces from "melting."

Buttonhook - A buttonhook is a tool used to facilitate the closing of shoes, gloves or other apparel that uses buttons as fasteners. To use, the hook end is inserted through the buttonhole to capture the button by the shank and draw it through the opening.

Acknowledgments

To the folks at the Historic Carson House... Dr. Jim Haney and the late Sara Bryant... Your tireless efforts to preserve, maintain and treasure the "house" is a tribute to the Carson family and their descendants. Thank you for your patience with me as I asked hundreds of questions. Your input to my research was priceless, and your kindness and encouraging words were a blessing. I am grateful.

To Carly Kauffman... God knew. Our meeting was no accident. Thank you for your beautiful illustrations. You captured the images in my head perfectly. You are a precious friend to me and I appreciate your tireless work on this project.

To my family and friends... I could not imagine my life without you. Thank you for your support, encouragement, and unconditional love.

To my grandsons... I love each of you so much. I hope this book will encourage you to cherish our family memories. The Word of God says, "For where your treasure is, there will your heart be also." When all is said and done, you will have your memories. May those memories be the treasures of your heart.

Made in the USA
Middletown, DE
04 April 2015